NEW VANGUARD 216

# SUPER-HEAVY TANKS
# OF WORLD WAR II

**KENNETH W. ESTES**          ILLUSTRATED BY IAN PALMER

First published in Great Britain in 2014 by Osprey Publishing,
PO Box 883, Oxford, OX1 9PL, UK
PO Box 3985, New York, NY 10185-3985, USA
E-mail: info@ospreypublishing.com

Osprey Publishing is part of the Osprey Group

A CIP catalog record for this book is available from the British Library

Print ISBN: 978 1 78200 383 0
PDF ebook ISBN: 978 1 78200 384 7
ePub ebook ISBN: 978 1 78200 385 4

Index by Fionbar Lyons
Typeset in Sabon and Myriad Pro
Originated by PDQ Media, Bungay, UK
Printed in China through Worldprint Ltd

14 15 16 17 18   10 9 8 7 6 5 4 3 2 1

Osprey Publishing is supporting the Woodland Trust, the UK's leading
woodland conservation charity, by funding the dedication of trees.

**www.ospreypublishing.com**

## ACKNOWLEDGMENTS

The author is indebted to many individuals and institutions. Timothy
Nenninger, Chief of Modern Military Records section, rendered the most
essential services of the US National Archives and Records Administration.
David Fletcher and Stuart Wheeler shepherded me through a pleasant
research visit at the Library and Tank Museum, Bovington, UK. Michael
Green and Steven J. Zaloga shared their personal archives and knowledge,
and along with Daniel Shepetus, also advised me over the years while this
project germinated. Thanks also to Josef Poslitur, Chris Hughes, Jason
Negri, Mike Verrall, Hillary Doyle, and Akira Takizawa.

## DEDICATION

Dedicated to Colonel Marshall "Buck" Darling USMC (1941–2004), my
second military mentor. He was a constant source of encouragement
and confidence.

# CONTENTS

# SUPER-HEAVY TANKS OF WORLD WAR II

## INTRODUCTION

Popular historical surveys treating tank development may reach back to war wagons and mobile forts once drawn by no less a visionary than Leonardo da Vinci, as well as early examples and improvisations dating from Muscovy and the Hussite Rebellion. Although tanks and tank warfare also may claim antecedents in chariots and cavalry arms of the ancients, modern tanks reflect equally the evolution of siege machines. The inescapable fact remains that tanks emerged as early innovations to break the deadlock of ground combat early in the twentieth century.

The super-heavy tanks of World War II owe their existence to the siege machine tradition. As a class of fighting vehicle, they began in the World War I concept of the search for a breakthrough tank. Without earlier improvements to the internal combustion engine, metal fabrication and rapid-firing weapons, their introduction would have been much delayed. The World War I Western Front provided the immediate military problem that caused their later development.

We will classify the super-heavy tanks as armored fighting vehicles of 70 metric tons or more, borrowing from the briefly expounded US Army 80 short-ton criteria of 1946. There was never an international standard. We should not be surprised that the breakthrough tank projects of the period prior to World War II took place in the armies suffering the greatest casualties of the Great War (Russia, France, Germany). Herein we find the progenitors of the World War II super-heavy tanks, worthy of mention in our introduction and concept development.

Although only the French Army had on hand some of these super-heavy breakthrough tanks at the beginning of World War II, the major armies sooner or later began projects aimed at fielding updated versions of them, as well as equally super-heavy tanks intended to dominate the armored battlefield. The latter category became the almost exclusive domain of the German Army as it operated under the twin pressures of its diminishing operational prospects in the war, plus the increasingly convoluted activities of the industrial leadership.

Although a very small number of super-heavy tanks were built or saw active World War II service in the armies of the major powers, it remains clear that their impressive appearance and specifications have captured the interest of armored fighting vehicle enthusiasts, pundits, and military personnel.

Once discovered, the search is on for more information. In many respects, this appeal stems from the engineering feats undertaken by these projects, where improvisations of auto or locomotive manufacture often sufficed for smaller fighting vehicles. The super-heavies exceeded the imagination of most contemporary tank users and designers and, even today, occupy the top shelf in the pantheon of tank and armored fighting vehicle history.

## DEVELOPING THE SUPER-HEAVY TANK, 1918–40

The first practical modern tanks, conceived and developed by the British Army, went into action on the Somme front on September 15, 1916. They were large rhomboid-shaped armored tractors that contained propulsion machinery, machine guns, cannon, and crews within a single chassis, protected against bullets and artillery shell fragments. Their peculiar shape enabled trenches of up to 2.44m to be crossed. The descriptive term "tank" was applied largely as a security cover for their development by the British and supplanted the awkward alternative term of "landship." Employed to cross barbed wire and destroy opposing machine-gun positions, they gained increasing success in the war when employed en masse, with accompanying infantry and artillery support. Hundreds of tanks saw action in the following years in the British and French armies, including some lighter, two-man models, some featuring rotating turrets for employing weapons. The Germans managed to field only a few dozen machines for lack of incentive and materials. Although the Allies developed faster machines, the tanks put into action remained, in general, walking-speed, limited-endurance fighting vehicles, tied to an infantry support role and serving as a form of armored battering ram or siege machine.

By 1918, both the German and French armies planned a new generation of tanks that would play a decisive role in 1919, each hoping to break the deadlock on the battlefield. The German General Staff took little

The K-Wagen remained very nautical in its arrangements, typical of early landships. The commander and his gunnery officer observed from his cupola (bridge) and issued orders to the two drivers/helmsmen, who had no vision ports of their own. He issued orders to his batteries of guns and machine guns to engage targets. They would have been transported by rail in sections of approximately 30 tons and reassembled a few kilometers behind the front. Its scale model is paired here with the conventional A7V, which would have borne the lion's share of action had the war continued for the German Army, supported initially by the K-Wagen. (Photo and models by Steven Zaloga)

The two K-Wagen breakthrough tanks neared completion at the Riebe Works in Berlin, 1918. Their characteristics: weight, 120 metric tons; length, 13m; width, 6.1m; height, 3m; trench crossing, 4m; armor, 30mm maximum (front and side). Armament: 4x 77mm fortress guns; 7x 7.92mm machine guns. Engine: 2x V-6 Daimler-Benz diesels, each 650hp. Speed: 8kph. Crew: 27. (Photo NARA)

interest initially in tanks, which had not proved decisive at the outset, and in any case the plan for 1917 was to defend in the West while the decisive moves took place in the East. However, improvements in the British tanks and the need to return to the offensive in the West provoked new policies in 1917. Their slowly evolving A7V was ordered into low-rate production in early 1917, but further efforts were ordered before it was ready. A supporting giant tank was proposed to augment the A7V, the GrossKampf-Wagen (K-Wagen), with a planned size of 150 tons, sporting four 77mm fortress guns and seven machine guns, and powered by two marine diesel engines. Finally, ten vehicles were ordered on June 28, 1917, taking shape as somewhat smaller vehicles of around 120 tons. Two bridge-building firms were contracted for their assembly, estimating a year to build. The track was adopted from excavation machinery.

In October 1917, they were re-evaluated by the General Staff as suitable only for static warfare, not exploitation. By the Armistice, two of the K-Wagen designs were nearly completed (one without engines) by Reibe Ballbearing Works at Berlin, and another neared completion at Wegmann Carriage Works at Kassel. The Germans dismantled all under close inspection of the Allies.

### Char 2C

The French Army mostly followed the guidance of General Jean Baptiste Eugène Estienne in the development and formation of its tank arm, leading, among many innovations, to the fielding of the FT-17 light tank, which had the first rotating turret and could be produced en masse as an infantry accompanying tank. Yet he also subscribed to a heavy tank concept, much heavier and more tactically focused than the *artillerie d'assault* vehicles, such as the Saint Chamond and Schneider. He saw the need for a heavy tank for every three to four light tanks as early as February 1917. The La Seyne (Toulon) shipyard of the Forges de Chantier de Méditerranée (FCM) already had heavy tank designs in development, and with the encouragement of Estienne proposed a super-heavy vehicle of some 68 tons, carrying a turret-mounted 75mm gun, armored to at least 35mm, capable of crossing trenches of 4.5m width. The ensuing political and military dialogue eventually produced a plan for 300 Char 2C in Plan 1919. The Armistice produced sharp markdowns in procurement, and only ten of the super-heavies would be funded.

Once in hand, with the last Char 2C delivered in 1921, the French Army had the unique position of having such vehicles for experimentation and subsequent development of doctrine for their employment. Because of its age

in 1939, the Char 2C may be mistaken for an antique artifact of a bygone era. However, a number of breakthroughs were achieved in its engineering. It ranks as the first operational tank to weigh 70 metric tons. Some other "firsts" include:

- Trench crossing in excess of 4m (4.5m achieved)
- Mounting a long-barrel 75mm in an armored turret
- Mounting an auxiliary machine-gun turret (for clearing trenches and rear protection)
- Mounting a machine gun in the hull front
- Engine power over 500hp
- Division of compartments: driver, fighting, and engine (the modern standard)
- Unique use of stroboscopic viewing devices for its turrets

The second FCM 2C to be completed, later named Picardy, on the grounds of the FCM shipyard. The four machine guns are not fitted, but the photo shows the unique cupola on the 75mm gun turret (and the rear machine-gun turret), which rotated at 300rpm inside a similar static cylinder giving stroboscopic vision to the occupant through the vertical slits, yet remained impervious to small-arms fire. (Photo Marius Bar, Toulon)

Although notions of heavy breakthrough tanks appeared in British, German, and Russian studies and plans between the wars, the French explored these concepts in greater detail. Thus during the period 1918 to 1940 the French Army pursued a program of heavy-tank development, beginning with the Char 2C of 70 metric tons, and analyzed lessons and experiences drawn from World War I. The conception and construction of the Maginot Line also played an important part in the development of a series of French heavy and super-heavy tank studies and designs. These emerging designs variously sought to fight enemy tanks, halt enemy breakthroughs, assault enemy fortifications, and fit into the scheme of French defensive works, such as the Maginot Line. Studies initially worked around a specified maximum weight of 45 tons, but this factor increased because of additional armament and armor. By the late 1920s, the designs of *chars de forteresse* (fortress tanks) called for 100-ton machines protected by 100–150mm armor plating and mounting high-velocity 75mm cannon. By 1938, the requirement for 90mm cannon capable of firing against the embrasures of fortifications and employing flamethrowers entered into play. Various designs included

The FCM 2C required no disassembly for rail transport, although the forward cupola was dismounted in this instance for overhead clearance. The specialized rail transport bogies permitted this, on flat and stable rail lines using four 35-ton hydraulic jacks, dunnage, and other support gear. (Photo Marius Bar, Toulon)

a skeleton tank, an articulated tank, paired cannon, the installation of two turrets, a tank capable of being disassembled and transported by train, and a tank mounted on railway bogie wagons. The coming of World War II then caused some rapid decisions, and many proposals for tanks weighing 140 or even 220 tons therefore did not get off the drawing-board. On April 13, 1940, the eighth meeting of the Commission on Fortress Tanks convened, viewing proposals from industry, and immediately ordered ten vehicles from FCM, designated the F1, to be ready for operations in May–June 1941. The events of June 1940 made the order superfluous.

This action, however, did most likely explain the strange odyssey of the old FCM 2C tanks, of which only eight were capable of further service in 1939, once re-engined with Maybach engines that had been held in storage since they were taken as reparations in 1919. At first kept for possible offensive operations against the Germans in the event the Poles held off the initial German attacks, such deployment was canceled and the 51st Tank Battalion continued training using the FCM 2C, likely to maintain cadre for new super-heavy tanks expected to be produced during the war. When ordered to evacuate to the south by the Third Army, two tanks out of repair had to be destroyed on June 13, 1940. The remaining six were rendered unusable days later on their rail undercarriages, caught in the general withdrawal without their locomotives in a defile with no chance of offloading. They were later hauled off to Germany as trophies and salvage.

### Initial Progress to 1940: Design and Specifications of Super-heavy Tank FCM F1

The FCM F1 order never progressed beyond the full-scale wooden mockup the manufacturer had demonstrated to the commission in order to win the contract. It does present a benchmark for the continued evolution of this type of vehicle, however, in terms of technology and engineering. A true "land battleship" weighing 139 metric tons combat-loaded, it featured two turrets oriented to its various missions. The primary turret, raised to permit 360-degree rotation, carried a variation of the naval DCA Model 1926 90mm/L50 (L=barrel length in calibers) antiaircraft gun with 88 rounds of ammunition. It was considered capable of sniping the weapons embrasures of enemy forts, thereby knocking them out of action. This was a remarkable feat, considering that the characteristics of the German West Wall forts remained unknown to foreign intelligence.

The second turret carried the Model 1937 47mm antitank gun, with 100 rounds. This would have been the weapon of choice against tanks in the fortress-tank mission of stopping breakthroughs or operating in the intervals of the Maginot Line. Mounted forward, it had a blind zone of about 100 degrees of its rearward arc. Six 8mm Hotchkiss machine guns rounded out the weaponry: dual mount in the bow (30-degree arc), one each side (30-degree arc), and a gun in each turret. Armor protection averaged 100mm all around (sloped frontally) to a maximum of 120mm. The crew of nine men (three fewer than that of the Char 2C) operated the weapons, radios, and the two 12-cylinder Renault KGM gasoline engines of 550hp each, which powered the Alsthol electrical drive system. Endurance of 200km on roads was planned, providing the 20kph top speed was sparingly used. As in the case of the smaller Char 2C, rail transport required the use of special bogie-heel assemblies to which the tanks were joined at each end via hydraulic jacks. Accordingly, these tanks also had relatively narrow hulls because of required rail transport conditions.

Had France managed to stop the German offensives in 1940, and had stalemate ensued as in 1914, the FCM F1 tanks could have entered service the next year, six months in advance of the first appearance of the German Tiger heavy tank. Together with the improved versions of the Char B heavy tanks and the Somua medium tanks, the French Army would have ironically fielded and operated the most modern tank force in the world during 1941–42.

# WAR AND THE TANK PROGRAMS, 1939–45

The opening moves of World War II in Europe in 1939 brought to an end the period of experimentation conducted in the preceding decade. The German pattern of the all-arms formation of tanks, mechanized infantry, engineers, artillery, and motorized logistic support, supported by tactical air power, became the new standard for the major warring powers.

Developments of tanks and their components now settled upon three distinct classes of evolution: the light, medium, and heavy tank, of approximately 10, 25, and 50 tons. Although armies had expected the antitank guns to dominate the battlefield as they had in the Spanish Civil War, tank mobility, armor, and firepower had advanced sufficiently by 1940 such that a new paradigm operated. Instead of the machine guns and light cannon of the previous decade, tanks in World War II carried main guns of up to 152mm bore, numerous machine guns, and even flame weapons or rocket launchers on occasion. Improved running gear and specially designed or modified engines permitted speeds in excess of 30kph. The armor protection by the end of the war exceeded the penetration power of all but the most unwieldy and heavy antitank artillery. Tank cannon now had to penetrate the armor of their opponents, and a number of specialized vehicles emerged for direct-fire support (assault guns, close-support tanks), antitank missions (tank hunters or tank destroyers), reconnaissance, engineering, tank recovery, and antiaircraft roles.

Most importantly, the operational doctrine for tank employment began to exploit not only the tank, but also accompanying mechanized troops of all arms, supporting aircraft and a fluid command style that permitted the exploitation of breakthroughs or weaknesses in the opposition forces, so that systemic collapses could be inflicted upon whole field armies. This doctrinal concept of rapid warfare, developed during the 1920s by the German Army, took advantage of tank and mechanized equipment developed in the 1930s to effect quick results on the battlefield not feasible in the previous era of foot and horse-mobile armies. Through 1941, the German concept, dubbed *Blitzkrieg* in foreign quarters, worked well as long as opponents could not manage to respond to German maneuvers or attack their vulnerable logistics.

## TOG Super-heavy Tanks

The British Army staff recognized at the outset of World War II that its tank arm had stagnated despite some theoretical progress achieved via experiments undertaken in the 1930s. Even as wartime production began to take form, the new Ministry of Supply sought novel designs and ideas to counter the obvious German advantages demonstrated in the campaign against Poland.

Even before the outbreak of war, the Secretary of State for War, Mr. Leslie Hore-Belisha had invited Sir Albert Stern to discuss mechanized warfare evolutions since 1918. On September 5 he notified Stern, who had headed the original Landship Program that developed the first British tanks in the previous war, that he welcomed his "suggestion to explore the possibility of designing and constructing a special tank."

By then 62 years of age and having returned to his banking profession, Stern reactivated many of his previous associates to join his new committee, including naval constructor Sir Eustace d'Eyncourt, Major General Sir Ernest Swinton, engineer Major Walter G. Wilson and Sir William Tritton, the last

### CHAR 2C IN BATTLE, 1940

In September 1939, the eight operational FCM 2C were held ready in the fortified region for defense of the Maginot Line intervals during a German attack or to attack enemy fortifications in the event the Poles held out and an attack on the Siegfried Line in the Saar Region became necessary. However, engine problems and the deterioration of their electrical wiring made almost any movement a complex operation. In the fighting of June 1940, the high command moved the vehicles out of the fighting front.

But in this hypothetical situation, Third Army has ordered the 51st Tank Battalion into action on June 14, 1940. Near Gondrecourt-le-Château, seeing elements of French cavalry tanks retreating southward, Lieutenant Colonel Fournet drove ahead of his six tanks in a sedan, and then stood aside as the lead tank 97 "Normandie" broke through the tree line and fired its 75mm gun into a pair of Panzer III medium tanks with devastating effect as the Panzer II light tanks scurried for cover and concealment and the other five giants arrived. The victory was short-lived, however, as German Stuka dive-bombers came upon the scene and three of the Char 2C were left behind, in ruins. Nevertheless, the crews were elated at finally having a chance to rub out several panzers.

The 70-ton Char 2C carried a crew of 12 men. With dimensions of 10.27m long, 3m wide, and 3.8m high, it crossed trenches of 4.25m, climbed obstacles 1.7m high, and forded 1.4m streams. Maximum radius of action was 150km and maximum speed 12–15kph.

Armor consisted of 45mm front, 22mm side, 13mm top, 10mm bottom, 35mm forward turret, 22mm rear turret.

TOG1 demonstrates its excellent trench-crossing capability at the Foster's plant. The side sponsons are not mounted, but were originally intended to house a 2-pdr gun and Besa machine gun each, but later a turret was added, making these unnecessary. (Photo The Tank Museum, Bovington)

an engineer and chairman of William Foster & Co, the firm that had produced the first British tank prototype, Little Willie. Wilson and Tritton had designed and developed the first Mark I tank prototypes and production versions, initially undertaken by the William Foster firm in 1916.

After visiting France, the group formally convened under the Ministry of Supply on October 12, 1939 as the Special Vehicle Development Committee (SVDC), but because of its origins quickly dubbed itself "The Old Gang." Its charge was to act upon a specification "RBM 19" of the Imperial General Staff dated September 28, 1939 for a "super-heavy tank (land battleship)" designed to operate in France on the old World War I battlefields and in the same conditions. The details included immunity to 47mm antitank and 105mm howitzer shots at 100m, and carrying a field gun capable of penetrating 2.13m of reinforced concrete, along with two standard 2-pounder (weight of shell,

The main armament of TOG1 was to be the most powerful field gun that could be mounted in a hull casemate. By default, the French 75mm field gun was adopted, but what TOG1 actually carried at this point was the 75mm casemate gun of the French Char B1 heavy tank, brought back from a visit by Stern, who jealously guarded it. (Photo The Tank Museum, Bovington)

The sole TOG2 prototype with its penultimate turret for the 3in 20cwt antiaircraft gun, fitted with a proper mantlet, coax machine guns, and periscopic sight. A 2in smoke mortar would have been mounted on the left side of the top as well. This is the form the TOG2R production version would have taken for use in the Middle East. (Photo The Tank Museum, Bovington)

common UK nomenclature) tank cannon, four machine guns, and four smoke mortars. The requirement included a diesel engine capable of 8kph for 80km endurance. The tank had to cross trenches 4.88m wide and climb obstacles 2.13m high and not exceed a ground pressure of 0.35kg/cm².

True to form, the committee had its preliminary design in hand by late December, with a wooden mockup. Because of the power requirement, a new model diesel engine of the Paxman-Ricardo type developing over 600bhp was needed and would be coupled to an original electrical drive that would alone bear the forces of weight and power and eliminate the problems of gear changing and mechanical transmission design that were foreseen. Two pilot models were ordered, TOG1, which was later converted to a hydraulic transmission variant TOG1A, and the second model, TOG2, with its tracks brought mostly inside the hull-side armor. Initially, the tracks had no suspension system, but moved over rollers. The same two pilots would be rebuilt several times in ensuing years as their designs changed.

Because of the focus upon tracked-vehicle experiences in Flanders during World War I, the TOG designs emphasized the need for low ground pressure, vertical-obstacle and trench-crossing performance, heavy armor, and a powerful tank cannon. When no gun capable of tank use could be found that pierced the specified 2.13m of concrete, the ubiquitous French 75mm field gun was chosen as next best, to be hull-mounted in front. The use of sponsons for the 2-pdr and machine guns was later rejected as too ungainly and instead a conventional (Matilda II) tank turret and side-mounted machine guns would be installed.

The resulting tank design under construction for an October 1940 delivery by Fosters now weighed 68 metric tons. Armor by this point was 3in (76.2mm) all round. By using 0.84m track plates, a ground pressure of 0.61kg/cm² was achieved. Thanks to its length of 10.52m and track height of 2.13m, it would cross a 4.5m trench and climb a 1.66m obstacle. With its width of 3.05m, the tank would remain transportable by rail without disassembly.

Trials undertaken by the TOG1 in November 1940 demonstrated overheating problems for the electrical transmission, as well as difficulties with steering because of the extreme length-to-width ratio of the hull and tracks. When the transmission caught fire, the committee decided to rework TOG1 and fit it with a Sinclair hydraulic transmission. The resulting TOG1A was running well in June 1943 at 11.14kph when final drive weaknesses again threw the design into doubt. Its final test run in December 1943 produced track roller failures, and that terminated its activities after 271 engine hours of total operation. On August 21, 1944 TOG1 was shipped to Chobham on a 100-ton transporter. A letter of July 14, 1947 reported that its engine and motors provided variable speed drives for test beds.

The TOG2* version of the prototype at Bovington demonstrates the unique descending upper track, angling down from the front idler wheel to pass under the turret floor for added protection. The upper line of rivets on the right side of the photo shows the track passage to horizontal. (Author photo)

Work on the second prototype, the TOG2, began on June 27, 1940 at Fosters. It was delivered in March 1941. The main difference in this design lay in the reduced vulnerability of the tracks rendered by dropping them from the front idler wheel to a level below the fighting compartment, leaving much more internal room and at the same stroke placing the upper track behind the side armor. Secondly, the main armament was placed in a turret instead of the hull. The propulsion system remained diesel-electric drive. Sponsors for mounting additional guns were again considered but later dropped. However, for rail transport, the larger turret required dismounting for vertical clearance.

This view of the rear deck of TOG2* at Bovington demonstrates the huge size of the engine compartment, made necessary by the designed diesel-electric propulsion and steering system. The openings for cooling and engine exhaust (nearest camera) were covered by heavy gratings. (Author photo)

Four turrets were developed for the TOG2, initially to mount the 3in antiaircraft gun, but the last for the 17-pounder (76.2mm) antitank gun, plus two coaxial Besa machine guns. Depression was -10 and elevation +20 degrees. A 2in smoke mortar was fitted to the left of the gun mount. The 17-pdr gun was probably an overmatch for the tank, despite its size. When on an 11-degree slope, neither hand nor electrical drive could traverse the turret. Ammunition carried was 85–100 3in shells, 4,800 rounds of 7.79mm Besa, and 30 2in bombs for the mortar.

The committee planned on producing the TOG2 for immediate use against the Axis ground forces in North Africa. Designated the TOG2R, the production version weighed 61.7 metric tons. A document signed on November 26, 1941 estimated the cost of air filters for TOG2R, using equipment already in use in the Middle East for tanks and armored cars.

Stern submitted a "Note on Heavy Tanks" to the Army Tank Board on June 13, 1941, criticizing inadequate preparation for the future. The army

The driver's and vacant machine gunner's positions illustrate the unusually large internal volume of TOG2, reminiscent of a submarine compartment. The turret basket to the left is the heavier version provided for the 17-pdr cannon in the TOG2* on exhibit at Bovington. It could not be traversed on slopes of 11 degrees or more from level. (Author photo)

continued to order more infantry and cruiser tanks. He had warned the Prime Minister in April 1940 that only such out-of-date tanks would be available for fighting in 1941. Now, none of them could carry the 6-pdr (57mm) gun. The SVDC had continually advocated the 6-pdr tank gun but, in July 1940, the General Staff protested against mounting this gun. The guns had now been ordered and there were no tanks to carry them. The SVDC had produced the TOG2 weighing 62–80 metric tons, which would carry heavier armor than any known tank and a high-velocity gun twice the size of even the 6-pdr (either the naval 12-pdr [7.62mm] or the 3in). It was specially designed for rapid manufacture, with the capability for at least 50 TOG2s to be produced for the campaign of 1942, and probably more like 100.

First it had to pass acceptance testing, however. This process began on July 2, 1941 at Farnborough. The vehicle was prepared for all but the 500-mile reliability test, because the track was not in proper condition after preliminary runs and demonstrations. The vehicle weighed 51 metric tons with its wooden turret. Matching vehicles in the test were Valentine and Matilda Mk II infantry tanks.

The TOG2* received a torsion bar suspension in April 1943. The failure to design a proper suspension for TOG tanks from the outset decisively damaged the prospects for development of operational versions, because of consistent failure of its components under vibration in trials. (Author photo)

TOG2 arrived overnight and was driven to the test site and fueled. That afternoon the Tank Board arrived and the test began. The TOG2 crossed two infantry trenches that could not be crossed by either of the infantry tanks: a 3.66m-wide trench and a combination of trenches. It then negotiated the official tank trap with the "greatest ease." A point-to-point race then ensued over a half-mile course of rough ground. The two infantry tanks covered it in 1min 30sec and 1min 45sec, the TOG2 in 2 minutes. The two infantry tanks then were stopped by a trench, the Valentine throwing a track. TOG2 completed the course and later

TOG2, as delivered by Foster's, also shows the rivet line of the track top, as well as the idler wheel track tension adjuster link on the side front. The side ports originally supported weapons sponsons which had finally fallen out of favor. Note the length of the tank behind the sponson, indicating the volume required for the propulsion plant. (Photo The Tank Museum, Bovington)

breached barbed wire that was thought capable of throwing the tracks of the other tanks. TOG2 and the Matilda II then completed the 2-mile cross-country course without mishap, although TOG2 needed a 30min break to cool down its electric motor temperature, which had reached 40 degrees Celsius. The next day saw hill climbing and tarmac top-speed tests, and on a downhill run the brakes failed and the vehicle reached 24kph. Amid the smoking engine compartment, mechanics discovered that an electric motor had exploded with considerable damage. A new braking system was designed for TOG2R.

The next field test at Farnborough took place January 1, 1942, with TOG2R tested against Matilda II and the new Churchill tank (A22). Essentially all three tanks performed well, but the TOG2R was bested in every category except for trench crossing. Time had caught up with the TOG2R and newer components for steering, braking, transmissions, and hydraulics were available that made the heavy and cumbersome diesel-electric plant of the TOG questionable. Moreover, the appearance of the Rolls-Royce

The first version of the TOG2 turret displays the two Besa machine guns as well as the 3in gun. The length-to-width ratio of the hull is most apparent, and it produced difficulties with steering during trials in soft ground or mud. That ratio, forced by rail restrictions, bedeviled most conventional tanks of the super-heavy class. (Photo The Tank Museum, Bovington)

Meteor tank engine offered significant power-to-weight advantages over the Paxman-Ricardo diesel.

On April 23, 1943 Churchill asked that 200 (preferably 400) Churchills be fitted with the heaviest armor possible with at least 100 pushed forward as an emergency. At the same time, he referred to the experimental development of a heavy tank at 60, 70, or 80 tons and asked for a report on the "Stern tank." On May 3 the Tank Board determined that the Stern tank had nothing to offer by comparison to the Churchill's progress. Instead, it was proposed that the super-heavy tank be studied for any technical improvements of value. It

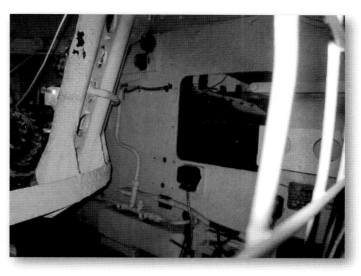

Continuing to the rear in the fighting compartment, the bulkhead behind the turret forms a firewall to the engine compartment, with the Paxman-Ricardo diesel visible. The repositioning of the generators to transverse positions would have saved 2ft of engine compartment length in a follow-on TOG2A, never accomplished. (Author photo)

bode no good for the TOG series that a few months later, a German Tiger tank arrived from Sicily almost intact and ready for exploitation. Reports described it as a 58-ton tank with a fluid-drive transmission with hydraulic couplings and hydraulic "steerage." The transmission control was by pre-selected hand-operated change of speeds.

Based upon a final trial in May 1944 of the 80 metric ton TOG2* (pronounced "TOG two star"), upgunned with the 17-pdr cannon and fitted with torsion bar suspension, the Department of Tank Design officially closed the TOG2 project because of the steering problems that had plagued the design since 1941. Shipped to Chobham on June 2, 1943, it is the same tank that rests today in the Tank Museum, Bovington.

A proper epitaph came years later from Vernon Cleare, a Merritt-Brown engineer who worked in British tank development from 1932 to the mid-1960s. "That the TOG vehicles were permitted to be built was an extraordinary thing and illustrates how Churchill was vulnerable to persuasion by some of his World War I associates. They were designed and built independently of the established tank design and development channels and were quite impractical for the situation in World War II. The vehicles were a complete waste of money, time, and effort and I never cease to be amazed that it was allowed to happen."

## KV-4 Super-heavy Tank Project
Between the wars, the Red Army design bureaus occasionally studied heavy tanks approaching the super-heavy category, but found no basis for using them beyond the theoretical breakthrough tank. In the events that followed, their heavy-tank developments generally provided such functions, although with design weaknesses. Because the early years of the Russo-German War were so closely fought for the essential survival of the Soviet Union, there was little choice in priorities for the tank industry but to maximize production of the existing models of light, medium, and heavy tanks, with only the most fundamental upgrades.

Certain wartime projects for super-heavy tanks existed, however, principally because of the experiences of the Russo-Finnish War of 1939–40 and the difficulties experienced in overcoming Finnish resistance despite

Russian superiority in numbers and equipment. In particular, the calls by General Kirill Meretskov for a heavy gun tank capable of destroying the reinforced bunkers his troops had encountered on the Mannerheim Line prompted several projects in the aftermath of the campaign, resulting in the KV-2 artillery tank with a 152mm howitzer mounted in an ungainly turret that overloaded the already problematic KV-1 heavy tank design. The design team of Zhozef Kotin turned to even larger heavy and super-heavy designs in a search for a solution. A KV-3, 4, and 5 series was undertaken, the first being an enlarged KV-1 heavy tank and the next two super-heavy tanks. The projects became complicated by the unwelcome intervention of Marshal Grigory Kulik, who headed the Red Army's Main Artillery Directorate. An uncannily misguided commander, who frequently misjudged military requirements, he had become convinced that the current tank cannon would be outclassed soon by the Germans, and he halted further projects such as an 85mm tank gun and forced development of a ZiS-6 107mm (F-42) cannon, which was not ready by the time the Russo-German War began.

The Kirov factory (Leningrad) of Kotin pursued the heavier tanks and managed to complete a prototype KV-3 hull, but no progress was made on fabricating the super-heavy KV-4 and KV-5 because of the conditions posed by the siege of Leningrad. However, Kotin did collect concepts and drawings from as many as 22 designers for the KV-4 super-heavy tank, which was conceived as a breakthrough tank that also could defeat any known German tank or likely successor. In these varied designs, the weights ranged from 86 to 108 metric tons and armor from 125mm on the side to 130mm on the hull front. All carried the 107mm main gun, and all but one design featured a secondary antitank gun of 45–76mm, plus two to four machine guns. All designs would use the M-40 diesel aircraft engine, rated at 1,200hp,

### B — BRITISH TOG2R

This TOG2R appears as it might have if deployed to Eighth Army in the Western Desert. Despite its weaknesses, the TOG2 could have brought a powerful gun and sturdy armor protection to the Eighth Army at a critical point in the 1942 North African campaign, particularly if the supply of M4 medium tanks by the United States had lagged. Accordingly, this planned production version, designated TOG2R, might have been assigned to the 50th Royal Tank Regiment, 23rd Armored Brigade, in late 1942. Weighing 62 metric tons, with 75mm hull armor, it would have carried the 3in gun (85–100 rounds carried) with a Besa coaxial machine gun in a turret protected with 75mm of armor on a 9.5mm shell all around, with a 38.1mm roof plate. Electric drive traversed it on the 1.68m turret ring and allowed -10/+20 degrees of elevation. The roof featured a 2in smoke mortar (30 rounds) left of the mount and periscope sights, with the commander's cupola copied from the A22 Churchill tank.

#### TOG2 Specifications

| | |
|---|---|
| Length w/o gun: | 9.53m |
| Width: | 2.97m |
| Heights: | to hull, 2.13m; to turret top, 3.35m; ground clearance, 0.5m |
| Tracks: | shoe 0.76m wide; length of track on ground with no sinkage, 3.2m |
| Performance: | can climb a 35-degree slope, and a 1.5m obstacle, and cross a 3.96m trench; top speed is 14.5kph |
| Range: | with 757 liters of fuel, it operates for 160km |
| Agility: | turning radius at speed is 9.1m, but remains capable of a neutral steer at halt |
| Crew: | six: commander, gunner, loader, driver, machine gunner, and assistant loader/radio operator |

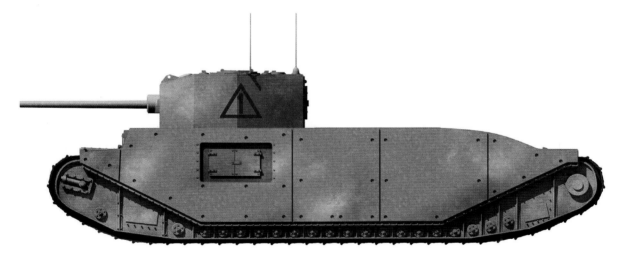

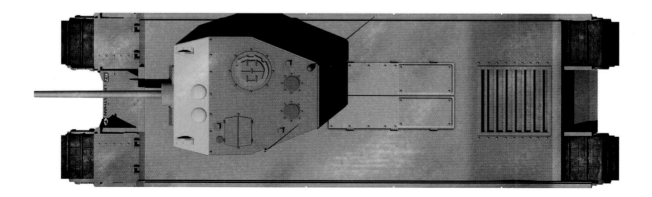

for a planned speed of 35–50kph. The 107mm ZiS-6 would penetrate 115mm of armor plate (sloped 30 degrees) at 1,000m. However, the Kirov factory had to cut back most production activities in the fall of 1941.

In the end, none of the 600 ZiS-6 guns produced on Kulik's orders equipped any tanks except for a KV-2 proving ground test rig, and all were scrapped because no tanks had been produced for them. The Soviet super-heavy projects were shelved as production waned at Kotin's Leningrad factory, and the tank plants built or transferred to the Urals concentrated on T-34 mediums and eventually the IS-series heavy tanks with which Russia finished the war.

## German Super-heavies

Unlike the British and Russian armies, the German Army faced tanks of superior size, armor, and firepower from the outset of World War II. Although their *Panzerwaffen* handled the Polish campaign with few technical problems, war with France meant confronting superior heavy and medium tanks such as the Char B and Somua, armed with 47mm high-velocity cannon that penetrated German tank armor with ease. French infantry employed antitank weapons in the same caliber and a portion of their 75mm field guns were detailed as antitank guns in support of frontline troops. Even greater challenges emerged with the Russo-German War, for the Germans had no initial answer to the KV-1 heavy tank and T-34 medium tank except for improvised use of the 88mm antiaircraft guns, and eventually improved ammunition for their standard 50mm tank and antitank guns.

Under a prewar requirement for a breakthrough tank, the Henschel Works eventually produced the 62-ton heavy PzKpfw VI "Tiger" tank that would not enter production until August 1942. Its first operational deployment took place on the Leningrad front in late September of the same year. The real response by Germany to the Russian tanks came with the fielding of 75mm antitank guns and the hurried design and production of the nearly 50-ton medium PzKpfw V "Panther" tank that entered service in May 1943.

Among the many effects of the Russo-German War, the successive technical shocks of superior tanks introduced by each side produced a gun-armor race that continued in some manner even after the war's end. For the Russians, their continuing requirement for mass production limited the ventures they could effectively undertake, and so they upgunned their T-34 to 85mm guns and replaced the KV series with IS-series heavy tanks carrying 122mm guns. Any further ventures had to await the end of the war, hence the abandonment of their super-heavy tank projects for the time being.

The Germans, however, placed a premium on technological quality and superiority over mass production, for which their industry (and, arguably, their regime) remained rather unsuited. Not satisfied with the advantage they obtained with the Tiger- and

The two prototype Maus hulls were shipped to Boeblingen for testing using specially designed heavy lift flatcars 27 meters in length and supported by 14 axles. (Author collection)

Prototype number 1 Maus began trials with a specially designed structure mounted to simulate weight of the turret. It is this hull that was taken by the Russians to their Kubinka Tank Museum after the war. (Author collection)

Panther-series tanks, the army leadership and Adolf Hitler himself pushed for larger and more powerful tanks than had ever been built.

## Maus

This tank project illustrated best the increasing influence of civilian contractors and political leadership upon German tank design and production that ran contrary to the previous well-established routine among army departments and contractors. The German Army bureaus acted on November 1, 1941 to the situation in Russia to specify a future super-heavy tank in the 70-metric-ton class. Because the Krupp Works had lost out on the Panther tank contract, the army approached them to pursue the project, stating an upper limit of 90 tons for the projected vehicle. In February 1942, with the situation in Russia deteriorating, the army awarded Krupp a contract for two VK 7001 prototypes in the 72-ton class with the 800hp Maybach HL230 engine, Tiger drive train and armor, and a 105mm/70cal gun. The intention was to go into series production as soon as the prototypes were delivered. In April, the project became the Löwe (Lion) tank, PzKpfw VII.

The same prototype returns to the tank park under the observation of Dr. Porsche (back, nearest camera). The vehicle's length-to-width ratio becomes clear. Steering in mud and soft soil was reportedly difficult. (Author collection)

Almost immediately, this tank project obtained Hitler's interest, and in conference with Armaments Minister Albert Speer on March 5–6, he directed Krupp to develop a 100-ton tank to be ready for testing before the spring of 1943. The designers created a 90-ton scheme beginning in April. However, by this time Hitler was convinced that the heavier Russian tanks would appear by that spring and that German tanks must be readied on a 100–120-ton basis. The Porsche firm had already received an army contract for a 100-ton tank in March, and in late June Hitler approved the drawings for the Porsche 100-ton tank, to be armed with either the 105mm or a new 150mm cannon.

Krupp was to build the turret and received the contract on July 17. The Löwe tank previously ordered by the army was canceled on May 18 (hull) and July 20 (turret). Both the Porsche and Krupp firms initially competed for an enlarged and heavier tank in the 150–170-ton range, carrying a 150mm and 75mm dual armament. By this point, the tank's concept had reverted to the old breakthrough tank role, so a slower speed and infantry support mission supplanted any particular notion of dueling with enemy tanks in a fluid battlefield, which would have taken place in any case as the war narrowed to the defense of the Reich.

The Krupp contract called for the heavy PzKpfw VIII Maus turret, but the army procurement officers had urged the firm to continue work on a lighter design that would make use of as many Tiger tank components as possible, in view of Professor Porsche's difficulties with his Tiger design, then in its final stages. This move also reflected the army bureaus' frustration with the meddling of industrialists and politicians in army procurement processes. The Krupp project received formal approval on November 10, leading eventually to the E-100 vehicle. Dr. Porsche presented his firm's drawings for a 170-ton tank on November 17, calling for a turret placed on the vehicle rear, with engine forward of it, generators under the turret, and electrical propulsion at the rear. The heavy armor included most of the suspension

## 1: BRITISH TOG1

One prototype TOG1 was built. Specifications are from the draft operator's manual (The Tank Museum Library, Bovington):

**Turret**: 1x 2-pdr (40mm), 1x Besa machine gun. Sponsons: 2x Besa machine guns each (30min to retract sponsons). Hull front: 1x 75mm gun, 1x Besa. Crew of eight (when sponsons mounted).

**Propulsion**: Paxman-Ricardo 12VTP water-cooled V-12 diesel, rated 550bhp at 1,500rpm, electric drive, 2x generators, 2x English Electric motors.

**Radius of action**: 96.5km on 757 liters of fuel. Air brakes. Speed on level: 11–13kph.

**Dimensions**: Length: 10.5m; Height: 2.13m hull top, 3.23m turret top; Width: 4.72m sponsons out, 3.05m sponsons in. Weight: 68 metric tons.

**Climb**: 40-degree slope at 1.6kph for 5min; 1.68m vertical obstacle. Crosses a 4.6m trench; holds side slope up to 40 degrees without turning over.

**Track shoes**: 92 each side, pitch 241mm, projection of shoes 62mm, link pins 32mm, weight of shoe and pin, 45.8kg. Ground pressure: 1.46kg/cm$^2$ on hardstand. With 305mm sinkage in soil, 0.61kg/cm$^2$.

A final proposal from the TOG committee for this vehicle would have made use of the Rolls-Royce Meteor engine, but still retained the electric drive, which they thought essential for such a heavy tank.

## 2: SOVIET KV-4

The KV-4 did not progress beyond the drawing board. KV-4 designs in Kotin's bureau mostly called for two turrets for main and secondary cannon, but by 1941 multi-turret tanks already were in disrepute. Given the difficulties of wartime production, this illustration presumes that Kotin chose the only single turret design, that of N. Tseits, for the KV-4 prototype. Furthermore, he rejected the cylindrical turret of that design in favor of a modified KV-3 turret as a further economy of effort. The specifications are:

**Dimensions**: Length: 8.35m; Width: 4.03m; Height: 3.62m; Ground clearance: 0.55m; Track bearing length: 6.05m; Combat weight: 90 tons. Crew: six

**Armor**: Hull: 130mm front, 125mm side, 125mm rear; turret: 140mm

**Armament**: 1x 107mm, 2x 7.62mm DT machine guns

A prototype could have been built in 1942. If it had been, perhaps it would have been either maintained in the factory or sacrificed in the defensive battles of Leningrad.

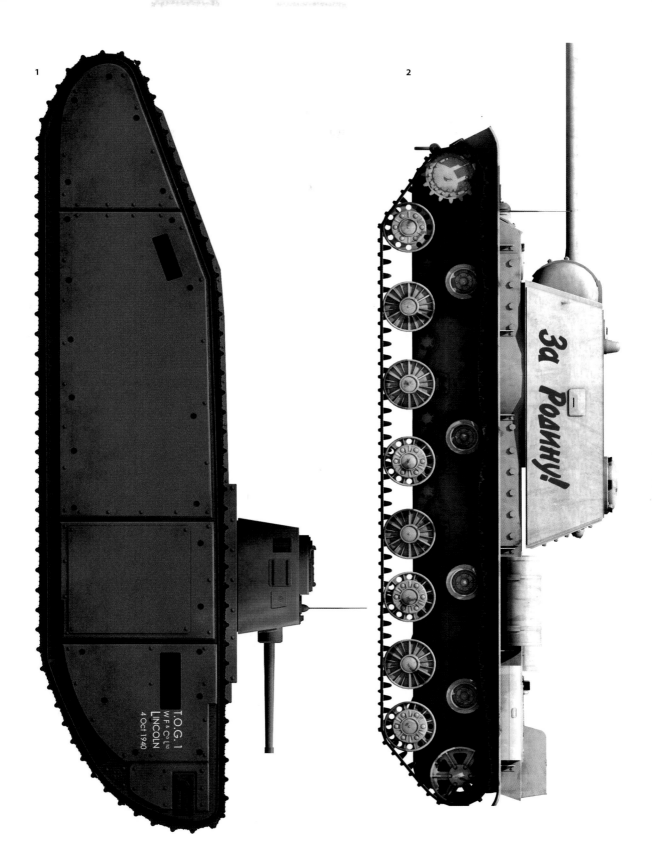

The frontal view of Maus number 1 demonstrates the high degree of frontal protection afforded by its design. The upper hull slope plate measures 200mm at 55 degrees; the lower hull center piece is 200mm at 35 degrees; tracks are protected by 100mm at 10 degrees. The turret face would have been 220mm of curved plate with a 250mm rounded mantlet around the barrel. (Author collection)

and track. Hitler ordered the Porsche Maus into production during a January 3–5, 1943 meeting, with an Alkett factory slated for the assembly of ten units per month for an eventual total of six prototypes and 135 operational vehicles. Hitler decided on the 128mm main gun, but ordered a turret finished with a 150mm gun for future consideration, with the current Krupp turret required to carry either (a measure canceled by the army in June 1944). Continuing Hitler's fixation with runaway technology, he professed that tanks in hand, such as Tiger and Panther for 1943, could maintain superiority only for a year, and Maus and the King Tiger (Tiger B) would therefore be required in 1944.

Design efforts culminated in the presentation of a full-size wooden model to Hitler on March 13, 1943. He had previously ordered the production of the first vehicle by May 1943, which would have frozen the design work effective that very March as he gazed upon the mockup. These measures proved too ambitious and in January the deadline for the first vehicle was reset instead to September 1943, with four more ordered completed by year's end. The desired production rate remained set at ten units per month.

Disaster twice struck the Krupp Works at Essen. A bombing raid on the night of March 5/6, 1943 destroyed the engineering worksheets and drawings for the Maus turret, and burned a wooden engineering mockup. The first turret delivery slowed from mid-October to at least two more months. The armored hull assembly line was unmolested. However, a second air raid in early August effectively killed the project. The first ten hulls survived but would take more time for finishing. The first two could be sent to Alkett once debris was cleared. Armor plates existed for another 30 vehicles. Turrets remained a different matter, however. The first turret was delayed until December by destroyed components, and no others could be worked on until such parts were located and the damaged armor works restored to operation. A later estimate delayed further hull and turret production for seven to eight months. In response,

The nearer KV-1 tank appears relatively large compared to the distant Maus on the testing range. The side armor of the latter demonstrated similar levels as the front: Hull: 180mm, at track level 80mm hull and 100mm skirt armor. Turret was 200mm at 30 degrees. (Author collection)

the army canceled production of the Maus on October 27 in order to concentrate on ongoing production of other vehicles. One Maus turret and two hulls would be completed and shipped to Alkett. This was the only known destruction of armored vehicle production by strategic bombing in history. All contracts were canceled or modified for the closeout by November 12. Despite feelers put out to restart production by industry leaders, the army gave permission on July 27, 1944 for Krupp to scrap the next four hulls that remained in its shops so as not to obstruct current production.

Krupp shipped the first Maus hull to Alkett on September 26, 1943. Alkett assembled its suspension and shipped it to Boeblingen on January 10, 1944 for testing. To make space for production of other vehicles, Alkett shipped its remaining parts for the second hull on March 7 to Boeblingen for final assembly. The lone Maus turret arrived at Boeblingen on May 3, 1944 and was placed on the second hull during June.

The first Maus hull ran its trials at Boeblingen with a weight structure mounted to simulate the turret weight and size. The chassis alone drove 5km from the railhead to the tank park without difficulty on January 14. The next day, with the turret weight structure, the vehicle steered well for 2km off-road, despite sinking a half meter into the clay soil. Later trials determined the turning radius as 14.5m at forward speed. With its electrical drive, a neutral steer could be performed when halted. The chassis forded streams 1m deep and negotiated banks of 45 percent successfully.

The second Maus arrived from Alkett on March 20, requiring finishing at the tank park. Its turret arrived from Krupp Works on May 4 and was installed on June 8. Manual traverse was attempted on a 10-degree slope, and it required 30kg of force to accomplish. Power steering was not yet available, but failed when energized in early July. Fuel consumption then was noted as 350 liters per 10km, although engine defects may have accounted for some of this poor performance. The flat track plates were considered unusable and cleated track was ordered as replacements. The replacement of the track in the tank park required six men and eight hours' effort. With the second prototype on hand, the evaluation of the powering of one tank through an electrical cable to another engaged in fording proved successful. On November 19, 1944, Krupp returned its workers to Essen on orders of the army procurement bureau, and further work on the Maus was

The prospects for more production of the Maus quickly faded after the Allies landed at Normandy, and the practically inoperable prototype number 2 and the only completed turret were destroyed in April 1945 as the Red Army approached Kummersdorf. The turret now sits atop the number 1 chassis at Kubinka Museum. (Author collection)

ordered to cease. Hitler had already ordered all development of tanks with heavy guns stopped on July 21, but the armaments industry had its own inertia. The two vehicles moved to the Kummersdorf testing facility before the end of the year, where they apparently remained non-operational. When

**D**

## 1: FRENCH FCM F1

The FCM F1 reflected the two decades of French experience with their fortress tanks. As usual, the limitations of rail transport required a long and narrow hull, relative to overall size. These limited several design options and made the length-to-width ratio a difficult prospect for steering and turning radius. As with the FCM 2C of 1919, this *Char de Forteresse* would have used the special rail bogie system for transport.

### Specifications

**Dimensions**: Weight: 139 metric tons; Length: 10.53m; Width: 3.10m; Height: 4.21m (3.74m less turret)

**Agility**: Ground clearance 0.45m; fording depth 2.33m; vertical obstacle 1.3m; trench crossing 4.5m

**Radius**: 200km on roads

Had the French continued in the war, the follow-up to this vehicle would have seen the development of a gun firing shells with 150–200kg of high explosive filler to destroy thick concrete fortifications, but such a piece did not yet exist. The Commission on Fortress Tanks thought that such guns of 135–155mm would be required for a new tank once this transitional F1 design had been placed into operation.

## 2: GERMAN MAUS

In the Maus design, the driver and radio operator remained isolated from the rest of the tank in the forward hull, using a single overhead hatch for entry and exit. The 75mm gun originally was to be the short 24 caliber gun from prewar, but the muzzle had to be extended to 36 calibers to keep propellant gasses out of the engine intakes on the hull top.

### Specifications

**Dimensions**: 9.02m chassis length; 10.085m overall with gun forward; 3.67m wide; 3.63m to turret top. Ground clearance was 0.57m. The main gun is 2.774m above ground (center of tube)

**Weight**: 188 metric tons (planned)

**Crew**: six

**Armament**: one 128mm/L55, one 75mm/L36, and one 7.92mm MG 34 machine gun (elevation -7/+23 degrees). Ammunition: 55 rounds of 128mm; 200 rounds 75mm

**Performance**: Max speed 20kph; radius of action (on roads) 160km; fording 2.0m (or with submersion kit, 6.0m); obstacle clearance 0.75m; trench crossing 3.48m

**Automotive**: Interim Daimler-Benz MB 509 V-12 gasoline engine developing 1,540hp at 2,500rpm; 2x generators, 2x electric motors, rear sprocket drive. Six paired sets of road wheels per side, coil spring suspension; track width 1.1m

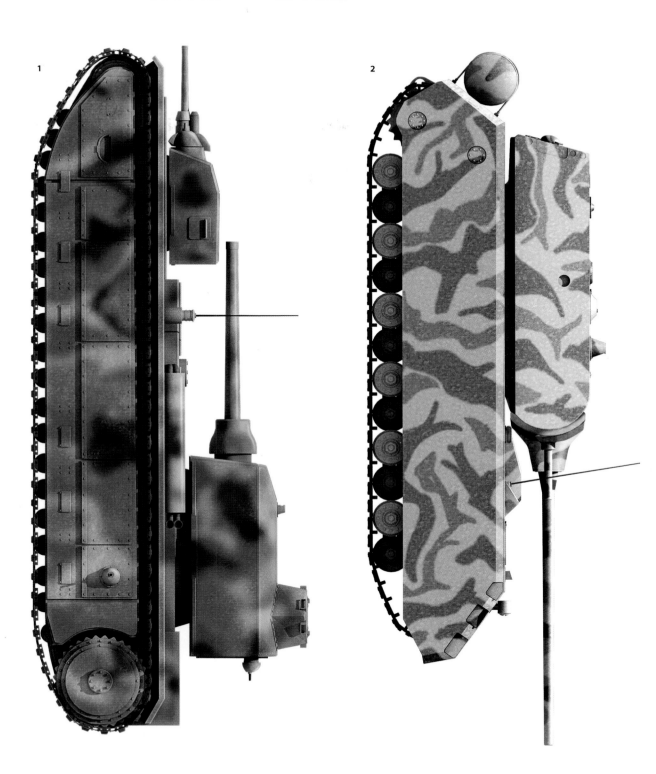

the Red Army approached Kummersdorf, the second vehicle with its turret was destroyed by the garrison. There remains no evidence of their use in combat. The Russians eventually placed the turret on the first prototype for testing and it now rests at the Kubinka Tank Museum.

## E-100

As noted in the Maus history, the army had encouraged the Krupp engineers to pursue a competitive Maus project in which Tiger tank components would be used to maximum effect in order to save weight, and improve reliability and performance. Although the Porsche design finally was designated the sole Maus project, the army managed to develop Krupp's Maus as the E-100 project. The Entwicklung [Development] Series of vehicles created by the army procurement bureaus ostensibly aimed at a series of fighting vehicles in successive weight classes that would share components and offer commonality of design as an overall economy measure. The reality remained that these designs frequently had no basis in the army program but were intended to dissuade the industrialists from using their access to Hitler and other leaders in order to press new programs that the army neither needed nor desired. At the same time, the E-Series vehicles demonstrated the requirement to limit further growth in external dimensions because of cost, weight, and transport penalties. Because the size and required number of projectiles also had increased during the war, the new designs freed more internal volume for such use by abandoning torsion bar suspensions in favor of externally mounted ones, and also by placing all engine/drive components in the rear hull, thus eliminating the power train extending through the driver's compartment. Only in the largest vehicle class, the E-100, was this last measure initially not feasible, although a new rear hull-mounted power pack remained with the designers as a future possibility.

Although the Krupp Maus design was adopted as the basis for the E-100 project, the army procurement officers did not think Krupp could add another such project to its manufacturing workload. Accordingly, the Adler automotive works of Frankfurt was designated as the contractor, working with the Army Weapons Office from June 30, 1943 to finish the pilot design, which they would assemble at Sennelager army base near Paderborn. Work progressed slowly, a sure indication of the priorities of the E-Series. By January 15, 1944, the army reported the chassis assembly at Paderborn was almost complete, but practically stalled because of delays caused by parts not arriving or related wartime difficulties such as misrouting. Only three Adler workers labored at that point at the assembly site. In particular, the Belleville system suspension spring units, combat track (1m wide), fuel lines, and transmission cover plate had yet to be delivered. The workers could complete neither the suspension assembly nor the electrical system in the driver's compartment.

The E-100 chassis as discovered by American troops at Sennelager in early April 1945 and prepared by the British for evacuation to the UK. The slack suspension demonstrates that the coil springs were not yet mounted. No turret had been provided by Krupp, but the project may have been abandoned in 1945. Its armament would have been the same as that on the Maus: 128mm/L55, 75mm/L36 or L24, and one 7.92mm MG 34 machine gun (turret elevation -7/+20 degrees). Ammunition stowage was not finalized. Armor was slightly reduced from Maus levels: Hull front 200mm upper at 60 degrees, lower 150mm at 50 degrees, sides 120mm vertical, rear 150mm at 30 degrees, top deck 40mm and belly armor 80mm forward, 40mm aft. Turret configurations varied, and perhaps would have equaled Maus in the end.
(Author collection)

For lack of a better motor, the Maybach HL230 had to be installed as a temporary measure. Most serious, though, was the absence of a turret, for which the army report lacked information. Krupp had supposedly designed a turret for the E-100 by May 1944 that had saved weight compared with the one from their original Maus project of the previous year. It had thinner plates with a sloped front and mounted the 75mm gun on top of the 128mm gun, a most unusual arrangement.

Dr. Karl Jenschke, the technical director and chief constructor of the Adler Works, considered the E-100 an obsolete design once accepted. Postwar, he testified that rail movement required removing the outermost road wheels, outer sprocket and idler wheel rings, and suspension armor and then fitting transport track. He considered the proposed heavy armament of either a 150mm or 170mm gun to be feasible only as an assault gun variant, because the turret space could not accommodate loading such weapons. Krupp was supposedly manufacturing the turret, but had been delayed. A dead-weight unit would have served for initial trials.

The E-100 hull was captured in early April 1945 by advancing US troops. Little more had been accomplished and the suspension could not even mount the combat track that had finally arrived. There is no record of a turret being assembled for it and the project was likely abandoned.

## Jagdtiger
Ironically, the ill-fated Maus project did contribute to the sole German super-heavy fighting vehicle completed, and indeed the largest and most powerful operational one of World War II. The Maus specifications eventually centered upon a direct conversion of the 128mm antiaircraft gun, model FlaK 40, produced since 1942 by Rheinmettal-Borsig with a barrel length of 61 calibers. Krupp undertook the redesign, resulting in the 128mm PaK 44 antitank cannon, later renamed 128mm Panzerjäger Kanone 80, using a barrel 55 calibers long. No equilibrator was fitted and the resulting mounting remained barrel heavy, reducing the possibility of lengthening it for higher performance. Accordingly, no muzzle brake was fitted to avoid any reduction in muzzle velocity. The resulting weapon remained very fragile, and a folding travel lock as well as an internal gun lock was required to avoid knocking the weapon out of alignment. The army procurement bureau first approached the Krupp firm on February 2, 1943 with its proposal for a heavy tank hunter (Jagdpanzer) mounting the 128mm gun on the chassis of the King Tiger (Tiger B) heavy tank, slated for production by Henschel starting late that year. The concept of employment stated the need for an infantry-support weapon capable of fighting at ranges of 3,000m. Firepower and armor protection were given priority over mobility, although good

The face of battle: Jagdtiger No. X7, 1st Company, 512th Heavy Anti-Tank Battalion after being abandoned by its crew on April 1, 1945 at Obernetphen. This was the typical fate of super-heavy tanks lost by the Germans, as few of them faced decisive engagement. The frontal superstructure armor of 250mm at 15 degrees, front hull armor of 150mm at 50 degrees and lower hull armor of 100mm at 50 degrees made no difference in such cases. Hull rear was 40mm; rear superstructure was 80mm. (Photo US Army)

The same tank viewed from the flank. The Jagdtiger had all the same weaknesses of the King Tiger heavy tank upon which it was based. It remained severely underpowered, vulnerable to breakdown, and still vulnerable to fire through its 80mm side armor, inclined 25 degrees on the superstructure. The Henschel suspension consisted of nine overlapping road-wheel sets, using conventional torsion bar suspension, identical to the heavy tank. (Photo US Army)

off-road capability, including mud and snow, was desired. The orders at first called for frontal armor at 200mm. While Krupp held responsibility for producing the gun up to the armor attached to the gun cradle, also designing the required mantlet armor, the production of the vehicle rested with the Henschel firm. It would lengthen its Tiger B chassis by 410mm in order to accommodate the new design specifications.

Hitler approved the project on August 21, 1943 and Henschel had a full-scale wooden model ready to show him on October 20. Construction had already begun on the first hull at the Eisen Works at Orbadonau (Linz); it finished that November and was followed by three more the next month. Final assembly and series production began at the nearby Niebelungen Works (St Valentin) in December, and the first two vehicles rolled out in February 1944. They began the required testing for all vehicles at Kummersdorf on May 5, 1944.

**E** **GERMAN E-100 IN COMBAT, APRIL 1, 1945**

During World War II, the US 3rd Armored Division seized Paderborn after a pitched battle, March 31–April 1, 1945. This hypothetical depiction shows the E-100 in action with the turret somewhat different than the one proposed by Krupp for the E-100 in 1944. Although it saved weight, the idea of placing the 75mm secondary gun atop the 128mm gun in the turret would likely have failed any troop test and probably would have been discarded in the mockup stage for ergometric considerations. Thus the more conventional coaxial side mount would have been provided, perhaps using an original Maus turret among five found at Essen from the original lot and not yet scrapped. The Sennelager Base had served as a training and replacement center, and a number of trained tank crewmen were available, as well as ammunition. The Jagdtiger number 5 was disabled nearby; the crew took the ammunition from it and manned the E-100 that had been camouflaged and abandoned by the Adler factory personnel.

**Dimensions**: Length: 8.733m (incl. gun forward, 11.073m); Width: 4.48m; Height: 3.375m; ground clearance 0.50m. The main gun is 2.45m above ground (center of tube).

**Performance**: Max speed 23kph; radius of action (on roads) 160km; fording 1.65m; obstacle clearance 0.85m; trench crossing 2.9m

**Automotive**: Maybach HL230 V-12 gasoline engine developing 600hp at 2,500rpm; eight-speed OG 40 transmission, front sprocket drive. Eight sets of road wheels per side, coil spring suspension

**Weight**: 123.5 metric tons (planned)

**Crew**: six

After their review of the wooden model, the army bureaus had made several changes, some of them major. There would be no ports for firing submachine guns; separate loaded ammunition for the 128mm gun was finally accepted; frontal armor for the fighting compartment increased to 250mm; a 70-caliber barrel proposal was abandoned; and indirect firing capability was discarded.

On the other hand, some interruption to the production effort came from the irrepressible Dr. Porsche, who nominated the suspension system from his unsuccessful Tiger tank prototype that had been converted to a similar heavy tank destroyer. It consisted of four paired road-wheel trucks on each side, using a longitudinal torsion bar to stabilize each pair. Because of the simplicity and the external mounting of the suspension with simple screws, the Porsche suspension saved 1.2 metric tons and 450 man-hours of work on each vehicle assembly. It also saved some internal volume and raised the ground clearance 100mm, compared with the Henschel torsion bar suspension with nine road wheels per side.

Among the initial vehicles assembled, the first two delivered in February 1944 had the Porsche and Henschel suspensions mounted respectively. Testing during May revealed a serious vibration and pitching problems with the Porsche system, which abated only when exceeding 14–15kph on a hard-surface road. Shear forces could break the wheel units from the hull, and wheel loading increased track wear and breakage. The decision was made to manufacture only the Henschel version, but a total of 11 vehicles had to be finished with the Porsche suspension by September. This incident, as well as the ordered acceleration of PzKpfw IV medium tank manufacture at the Nibelungen Works, caused a certain delay in production that was not helped by a damaging bombing raid in mid-October.

Following the first two vehicles, the Nibelungen plant assembled three Jagdtigers each in July–August, then eight, nine, and six each following month until the record 20 delivered in December. On October 12, 1944 the army fixed the total order for this vehicle at 150, after which production would shift to Tiger B heavy tanks. Hitler intervened in January 1945, however, ordering production to continue and to accelerate if possible. The army hesitated

The Bovington Jagdtiger demonstrates the Porsche suspension system of four bogie pairs of road wheels, slightly overlapping and fitted with longitudinal torsion suspension for each bogie set. Although greatly simplified, it failed testing and was discontinued after a few vehicles were produced. The gaily colored tubes are cleaning rods for the gun. (Author photo)

to implement this command, and hedged it by ordering only 100 more from Nibelungen Works, transferring production in May 1945 to the Jung firm, which had no experience in assembling fighting vehicles. Some 88 of the Jagdtiger model were completed in all, with at least four fitted with 88mm cannon because of shortages. Most of the last eight likely never left the factory grounds and were supposedly destroyed before the Red Army took the plant on May 9, 1945. An example of this vehicle may be seen today at the Tank Museum, Bovington (with Porsche suspension), the Ordnance Training and Heritage Museum, Ft Lee, Virginia, and the Russian tank museum at Kubinka.

Technically, the Jagdtiger remained a highly advanced tank destroyer, fitted with a binocular gunner's periscope sight of 10x magnification with range scales of 0–4,000m and 0–8,000m for armor-piercing and high-explosive ammunition respectively. The 128mm/55 cannon penetrated 148mm of armor sloped 30 degrees at 2,000m and 167mm at 1,000m.

In operation, however, the vehicle displayed serious limitations because of its sheer size and mobility, frequency of breakdown, and difficulties in maintaining its armament in top condition. There is little doubt that the deterioration of logistic support and crew quality by the last year of the war contributed to some of these difficulties. However, the two battalions actually equipped with these vehicles suffered most of their losses from mechanical breakdown, lack of fuel, or bogging. Very few firefights took place, largely because of the difficulties of moving the tanks to the front in time for planned operations. Furthermore, the vehicles needed to be employed together in significant numbers because of their low rate of fire. The alignment of the sights and gun barrel needed frequent resetting because of the vibration they experienced, especially when operating without the travel braces in place. Even firing vibrations required frequent resetting of the sights. Engines and drive train did not hold up well on long marches. The driving characteristics

Despite the formidable armor of the Jagdtiger, this one, taken by the Americans to Aberdeen Proving Ground postwar, was knocked out of action after resisting several hits by tank main guns. None of them penetrated: the underside of the gun mantlet, the gouged lower hull center and on the hull side, just under the left front lifting eye. That last hit sprayed fragments into the left final drive unit, seizing it. The vehicle spun broadside to its opponents and the crew promptly abandoned it. (Photo US Army)

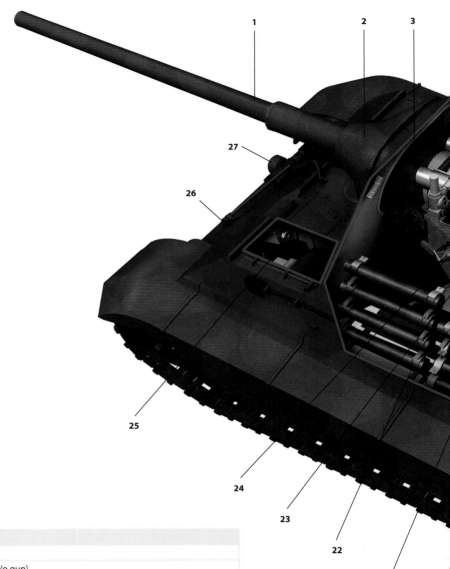

| Specifications | |
|---|---|
| Weight | 75 metric tons |
| Length | 10.65m (7.52m w/o gun) |
| Width | 3.63m |
| Height | 2.96m |
| Ground clearance | 0.49m |
| Track width | 0.8m |
| Main armament | 128mm gun; ammunition stowage 40 separate loaded rounds |
| Agility | ability to cross 2.5m trenches, ford 1.75m water, and climb a 0.88m obstacle |
| Range | 170km (on roads), with 860 liters of fuel |
| Top speed | 41.5kph |

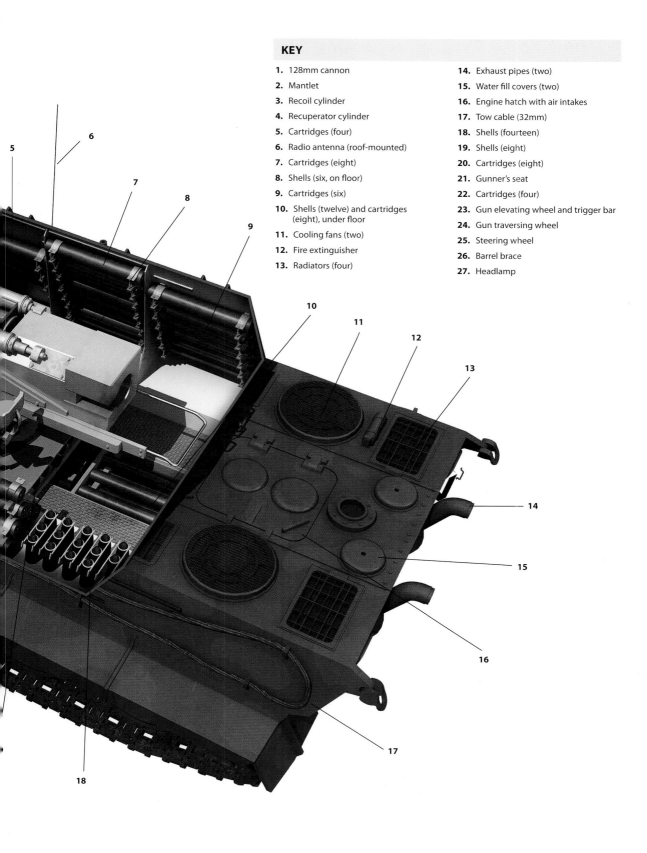

**KEY**

1. 128mm cannon
2. Mantlet
3. Recoil cylinder
4. Recuperator cylinder
5. Cartridges (four)
6. Radio antenna (roof-mounted)
7. Cartridges (eight)
8. Shells (six, on floor)
9. Cartridges (six)
10. Shells (twelve) and cartridges (eight), under floor
11. Cooling fans (two)
12. Fire extinguisher
13. Radiators (four)
14. Exhaust pipes (two)
15. Water fill covers (two)
16. Engine hatch with air intakes
17. Tow cable (32mm)
18. Shells (fourteen)
19. Shells (eight)
20. Cartridges (eight)
21. Gunner's seat
22. Cartridges (four)
23. Gun elevating wheel and trigger bar
24. Gun traversing wheel
25. Steering wheel
26. Barrel brace
27. Headlamp

This view of the Bovington Jagdtiger engine cover illustrates the limited volume available for the Maybach HL-230 engine. The compartments to each side held the gasoline tanks, radiators, and fans and fan drives. Deck armor was 40mm. (Author photo)

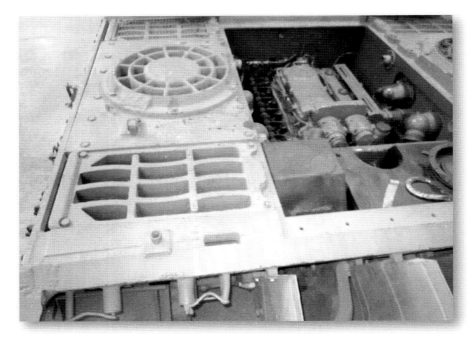

of these large, heavy vehicles proved especially challenging, and the lack of suitable bridges reduced the possibility of employing them on several occasions. Fording streams proved inadvisable because of the strain on the drive train and possibility of bogging.

Many of these defects may be considered teething problems given the hurried construction and issue to the troop units. However, they also represent the likely fate of the other tanks of the super-heavy class treated in this study. In a rush to achieve technological superiority over the opposing forces, the equipment quality actually fell far short of desired effectiveness simply because too few of the components could have been tested before incorporation in designs which themselves proved far too ambitious for the materials and engineering capacity of contemporary industry. One can sympathize greatly with the German Army procurement bureaus, which consistently sought to plan armored vehicle production for 1945 and onward simply in terms of numbers of Panther and King Tiger tanks, and lesser vehicles.

In the case of the German Army, the evident burdens on the bureaus could have only worsened had they attempted to build, let alone operate, the more fantastic and apocryphal concept designs that supposedly floated through the increasingly byzantine channels of their tank procurement. These fantasies include the projects called Ratte and Monster in the undocumented accounts that have passed through various internet and non-authoritative works.

The very idea that a tracked vehicle could be built to carry a battleship turret of the *Gneisenau* type with a pair of 280mm naval rifles, as suggested in the Ratte concept, exceeds most powers of belief. Quite simply, if one visits the surviving C turret of *Gneisenau* that the Germans emplaced for coast defense in the Austrått Fort at Ørlandet in the Trondheim region, the realities become apparent. The power supplies, magazines, and machinery required for such a turret would require far more than a 1,000-ton man-made object to simply support it in a static position. There is also a failure to record any likely justification for such a mobile weapon. If not a hoax, it very likely might have been an engineer's parlor game or other object of amusement. The same criteria apply to the "Monster," a concept for a self-propelled mounting for the 800mm Gustav/Dora cannon. The three to four railroad tracks required for the Dora gun and its personnel and supporting equipment already exceeded the rumored characteristics of this fantasy fully tracked device.

## Final Converts to the Super-heavy Category
### Japan's O-I

The development of the O-I and an earlier 100-ton tank by the Japanese Army reflected the basic requirement for building the strongest feasible tank, just as the Japanese Navy had worked on the world's largest battleship in the 1930s. The impetus for a 100-ton tank project stemmed directly from the defeat inflicted by the Red Army in the Nomonhan/Khalkin Gol incident of 1939. The army staff issued a top secret order for a "gigantic tank that can be used as a mobile pillbox on the great plains of Manchuria." In 1940 a 100-ton super-heavy prototype was built. Its general appearance resembled the Type 95 heavy tank. The main armament was a Type 92 105mm cannon, which had been tested before on the chassis of the older Type 95. Smaller turrets were present on both the front and rear of the tank, but their number was not yet specified. The suspension consisted of coil springs. After shedding its own suspension during tests, the 100-ton tank was canceled and the prototype scrapped. However, by 1944 the military situation for Japan had become desperate. Some information on super-heavy tank development in Germany came to Japan and that rekindled the idea of a new giant. Development restarted with a new super-heavy tank designated the O-I. The main armament in the central turret was once again the Type 92 105mm cannon, a modified field gun. Two small turrets topped the front hull, offset slightly left from the mid-point of the tank. One carried a Type 1 47mm antitank gun and the other a Type 97 7.7mm tank machine gun. On the rear hull, two similar heavy machine gun turrets completed the armament. Armor was a maximum thickness of 150mm. The suspension consisted of coil springs providing torsion to a bogie, suggestive of a modified Porsche road-wheel truck system.

The power plant consisted of two modified BMW aircraft type air-cooled gasoline engines, which gave a total of 1,100hp. This same modified engine was also used in the Type 5 Chi-Ri medium tank. The two engines were placed lengthwise parallel to each other in the rear. The structure of the transmission was the same as the Type 97 Chi-Ha, although the gears were heavy. The five-speed forward gear lever was in center front of the driver and both hands were used to adjust the lever. Like the 100-ton tank, the project was contracted to Mitsubishi, but due to the war situation the project was canceled before prototype completion. Weighing as much as 150 tons and crewed by 11 men, it fitted most aspects of the French fortress tank concept. Dimensions were: 10.1m long, 4m high (2.5m w/o turret), and track width 0.9m. Ground pressure was 1.20kg/cm². The two Type 98 550hp aircraft engines (modified BMW VI air-cooled V-12), produced a maximum speed of 24kph. The armor scheme involved turret armor estimated by some sources as up to 200mm all round, with front hull armor of 200mm thick, with sides 110mm or 75mm and 35mm plates added for a total thickness of 110mm. Weapons were one 105mm cannon, Type 1 47mm tank gun, and three 7.7mm heavy machine guns. The Type 92 cannon as a field gun was of 105mm/L45

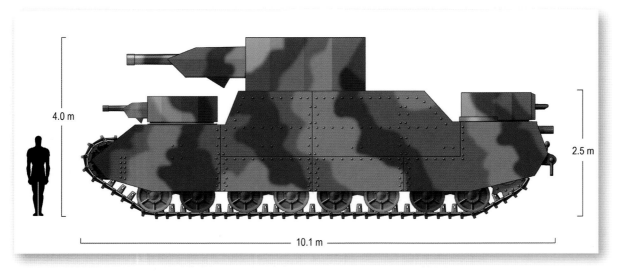

The Japanese O-I tank of some 120–150 tons represented the army's quest for some measure of equivalence to Allied armor in the war. How it could have operated in the limited capacity roads and bridging of either Japan or Manchuria defies imagination. Multiple turret design had been continued in Japan, and still seems likely as in this 1944 depiction, based upon a preliminary design, with the typical late-war camouflage. (Drawing by Steven Zaloga)

caliber, with 765m/sec muzzle velocity and a maximum range of 18,200m. The gun's high-explosive round weighed 16kg and the armor piercing round would penetrate 175mm of armor at 100m.

### The American T-28

During World War II, the US Army resisted most efforts to place a heavy tank into operation. The development and mass production of medium tanks were seen as the key to victory and the concept generally found satisfaction with the field commands. The difficult encounters with the heavy King Tiger and Panther medium tanks in Europe changed some of this policy, but the Army Ground Forces tended to oppose any tank approaching the 50–70 ton range. The Ordnance Department, however, saw a particular need for a special assault tank capable of dealing with fortifications once the Allies had established their armies ashore in France. In September 1943, concept and design work began on a vehicle designed to deal with the expected works of the West Wall and other conceivable German strongholds.

Early concepts called for use of the new T5E1 105mm cannon that performed very well against armor and reinforced concrete. With frontal armor 203mm thick, the resulting vehicle would require the electric drive installed in the T1E1 heavy tank and T23 medium tank. The Ordnance Department proposed building 25 such vehicles in time for them to be used

The T28, newly designated as a super-heavy tank, made an impressive appearance at this Aberdeen demonstration of October 3, 1946. Equipped with the most powerful tank cannon and heaviest armor of any US tank to date, it remained underpowered and arguably under-crewed (four men) for its intended mission. Gun traverse was 10 degrees right, 11 left. (Photo US Army)

after the invasion of Europe, advocating a sizable number of such vehicles in the event that enemy fortifications had to be overcome. Army Ground Forces did not agree and preferred the construction of three pilot vehicles using conventional mechanical drives. In March 1944, the design was approved for five pilot vehicles of the special assault tank, designated heavy tank T28.

Among many departures from conventional designs, this tank was designed without a turret in order to lower the height of an otherwise huge vehicle. The positioning of the gun far forward also allowed advantageous use of castings in shaping the hull against penetrations on front and sides. The 105mm gun would have at least 10 degrees of traverse to each side and elevation between +20 and -5 degrees. A crew of four was considered suitable for the vehicle: driver and gunner positioned to the left and right of the gun, and the vehicle commander behind the gunner. The loader worked in the left rear of the compartment. Only the driver and commander had vision cupolas, and the commander's included a 12.7mm machine gun that required him to stand in an exposed position. This was the only other vehicle weapon, so the

The davits shown on the preceding photo served to handle the unique outboard track-suspension set required to reduce the 86.2-metric-ton T28's ground pressure from 1.14 to 0.82kg/cm$^2$. When not required or for rail transport, the extra set was mated into a trailer configuration and towed. Side armor consisted of 64mm at 57 degrees on the cast superstructure and 50mm on the lower hull side, augmented by 102mm skirt armor plates. (Photo US Army)

With outboard tracks mounted, the T28 seemed relatively square in shape: 7.5m long (without gun) and 4.55m wide, but shrinking to a petite 3.15m with just the single set of tracks. Only the driver and commander had hatches, and the huge shrouded air cooling intakes and exhausts took the remaining space to the rear, supporting the 500hp GAF V-8 gasoline engine and Torqmatic transmission. (Photo US Army)

Protected by 305mm upper front armor and a 292mm gunshield for its 105mm/65 caliber cannon, the T28 proved a wartime exigency that disappeared almost as rapidly as it appeared. The gun fired a 33.6kg capped shot or a 27.2kg hypershot round at a muzzle velocity of 914.4m/sec or 1,128m/sec. A periscopic sight on top and the coaxial telescope were the gunner's aiming devices, and the only other weapon mounted was the 12.7mm machine gun for the commander. (Photo US Army)

T28 was clearly designed for engagements at a distance and under escort. The gunner had both periscope- and telescope-type sights. At his position to the left and rear of the gun, the loader also had a vision periscope. With a single loader and heavy separate loading ammunition, a rate of fire of four shots per minute was the maximum expected.

The engine provided was the same as that used in the M26 medium tank, leaving the T28 underpowered with a top speed of 12.9kph. In order to reduce the ground pressure, a second set of tracks was provided, with the 102mm side skirt armor included, and these were attached to the hull side in approximately 2.5 hours. When not needed or for rail transport, the extra tracks were linked together and towed as a trailer.

In January 1945, Major General Gladeon M. Barnes, chief of research and development of the Ordnance Department, advised the head of the department that the "startling performance of the new tungsten-carbide ammunition" now in use by the German Army left the T28 too vulnerable. He recommended increasing the frontal armor to 305mm. He confided that the Corps of Engineers was developing bridging capable of supporting tanks much heavier than 80 tons. Shortly thereafter, the Chief of Ordnance acted to change the designation of the T28 heavy tank to the T95 gun motor carriage because of its lack of turret and normal secondary armament.

The T28 climbs on its transporter at the October 3, 1946 demonstration. Without such support, it could sustain a speed of 11.3kph and on roads travel about 160km on its 1,514 liters of gasoline. It crossed a 2.9m trench, scaled a 0.61m obstacle and could ford 1.19m. (Photo US Army)

After some difficulty in locating a manufacturer not fully occupied with production, Ordnance contracted the Pacific Car and Foundry Company for the construction of the five pilots of the T95 in March. PacCar produced the first casting of the front end on June 20 and completed the welding of the first hull in August. Final weight was 86.2 metric tons, combat loaded.

The end of the Pacific War brought cutbacks to all ordnance programs and the number of T95 pilots dropped to two, with pilot number one delivered to Aberdeen Proving Ground on December 21, 1945 and the second one on January 10, 1946. With no need for breakthrough tanks or fortress tanks of any kind, the army used them for engineering tests at Aberdeen, Fort Knox, and elsewhere.

In June 1946, the vehicle was again redesignated under yet another army nomenclature change, now qualifying in the 80+ short ton range as the sole US super-heavy tank, T28. Testing continued at Aberdeen and Yuma Proving Grounds to determine wear of heavy tank components until late in 1947. Pilot vehicle two was lost to an engine fire and scrapped at Yuma. Pilot vehicle one,

This view of the upper hull shows the exhaust fan for the fighting compartment, the radio antenna, and driver's cupola. Note the interface between the castings of fighting compartment and engine compartment. Top armor was 38mm and rear casting 51mm thick. (Photo US Army)

assigned to Aberdeen Proving Ground, was simply lost in the records for many years, variously reported as destroyed or scrapped, until a conscientious lieutenant at Fort Belvoir conducting inventory wandered into a disused range in 1974 and made a most unusual discovery. Removed to Fort Knox for restoration and display, this odd surviving T28 now forms part of Fort Benning's National Armor and Cavalry Museum.

### Britain's Tortoise A39

The British Tortoise heavy assault tank forms a convenient close to this study, which for the World War II period began with the TOG and its similar origins.

The third prototype of the Tortoise shows not only the businesslike features of a powerful gun and thick armor, but also the extensive smokescreen equipment. The 2in mortar swiveled on the turret top, and fixed smoke dischargers mounted on the corners of the fighting compartment and the traversable machine gun cupola provided extensive self-screening. (Photo The Tank Museum, Bovington)

The British Army from time to time embraced the notion of assault tanks, which took the form generally of a conventional tank fitted with additional armor to resist the most numerous antitank guns of the German Army and allow it a chance to overcome prepared defensive positions and outclass defending armored vehicles.

None of these conventional assault tank schemes effectively dealt with the prospect of overcoming the German West Wall fortifications. Therefore, as in the case of the US, the British Army engaged in special development of a tank that exceeded all norms of size and complexity for that particular mission. The general concept was issued to industry in March 1943. The Nuffield firm undertook the contract for the A39 vehicle that took the name Tortoise from its shape and was the last of 16 concept designs reviewed in 1943–44 (two more concepts existed, but were heavy flamethrower vehicles). Once determined, the design was engineered and construction began on 25 vehicles for use in 1945. The progress of the war caught up with and passed by the program, and only six machines were completed, with deliveries starting in 1946.

**G**   **BRITISH TORTOISE**

The Tortoise heavy assault tank represented a return to the fortress tank concept of 1939, with the same specific challenge of the German West Wall in mind.

**Dimensions**: The tank measured 10.06m overall (7m without gun) in length, 3.89m in width, 2.87m in height.

**Performance**: Ground clearance was 0.38m and track width 0.91m. This vehicle crossed 2.44m trenches, forded 1.37m water and climbed a 0.91m obstacle. Ground pressure was 0.88kg/cm². Radius of action was 140km on roads, with 530 liters of fuel. Top speed was 17kph.

**Armor protection**: The fighting compartment consisted of a single large casting (15.88 metric tons) with 279–203mm at 0–47.5 degrees, 178–156mm sides at 85 degrees, and 120mm vertical rear. The hull front is 228mm, rounded; lower sides are 112mm; side suspension skirts 101mm. Rear engine compartment casting is 120mm. Top armor ranges between 33mm and 50mm, and bottom is 35mm.

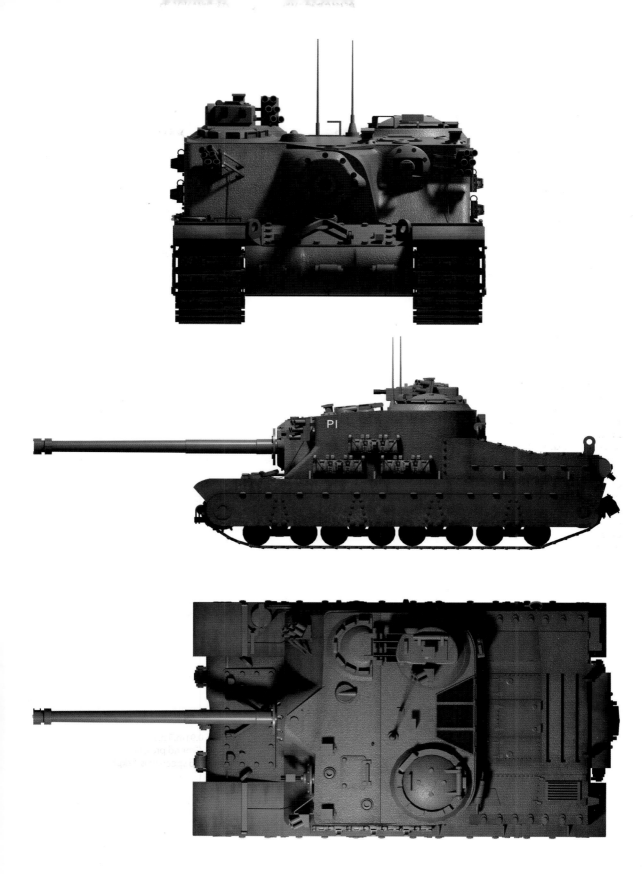

Prototype three again, here on its special transport trailer in 1948, performing the troop test in Germany. The troops especially liked the mechanical reliability of the tank and the power and accuracy of its gun. The less said about mobility in war-scarred Germany the better. By this time, a four-round projectile "clip" had been attached to the recoil guard, allowing a slim measure of ready ammunition. Although its service was limited, it ranks as the last of the super-heavies to have reached the troops. (Photo The Tank Museum, Bovington)

Reflecting the experience to date in World War II, the Tortoise design emphasized maximum armor protection and exceptional firepower, and accepted the low speed, mobility, and weight penalties that no other tank produced in the United Kingdom had been allowed to display. As with the contemporary US T28, a turretless design took shape, built around a very powerful gun not yet fielded in tanks, protected by massive armored hull and superstructure castings. A significant difference, however, was the provision of machine-gun positions that indicated more of a close combat role for this machine than its American counterpart. The provision of a tank-infantry telephone confirmed this intention.

The large single castings for the front hull (transmission gearbox) and superstructure (crew fighting compartment) and rear engine compartment were assembled into an all-welded vehicle, with a dual torsion bar suspension and 0.91m-wide steel pin track. Side armor plates covered the suspension to a very high degree. The main armament consisted of a modified Ordnance 3.7in/32-pdr (93.4mm) heavy antiaircraft gun, with a 62-caliber barrel length. The Rolls-Royce Meteor Mk V powered the vehicle with 650bhp at 2,500rpm, but even with a combat weight of 78 metric tons the top speed remained a somewhat respectable 19kph. Its radius of action did not exceed 140km.

A troop test in 1948 of two Tortoise tanks with the British Army of the Rhine proved the closest this tank came to operations. It was well liked for its mechanical reliability and firepower, but the weight and size of the vehicle made its transport and maneuvering simply too much to handle. As with all the super-heavies, the roads and towns suffered much ill-treatment.

Similar to its American counterpart, the Tortoise supported much ordnance and engineering study. Above all, the 32-pdr cannon provided interesting proofs for armor-piercing discarding-sabot ammunition of very high velocities. Proof firings in 1946 of a 1:1.76 subcaliber penetrator, the largest then attempted, produced muzzle velocities of 1,524m/s, slightly over the planned 1,448m/s. The sabot segments discarded out to 300m but the base flew over 1,000m, an evident troop hazard. The penetrations of 200mm homogenous plate succeeded at 1,280m/s at a 40-degree angle, but higher target angles produced shattering, indicating the need for much more research before attack with "superhigh" velocities could be attempted. The standard capped-armor piercing shot for the gun had much greater accuracy than the 20-pdr (84mm) with discarding sabot ammunition, and was even better at longer ranges.

Tests of the preproduction superstructure frontal and side protection in late 1945 against 17-pdr, 3.7in and German 8.8cm Pak 43 shots met all specifications of the design. Once the Brinell hardness had been reduced from 282 to 250–55, cracking problems ceased; the side armor resisted 17-pdr armor-piercing rounds, and the frontal armor resisted the 3.7in and 8.8cm ammunition at near-maximum velocities.

Stowage of ammunition remained problematic for Tortoise. None of the 60 projectiles had a ready ammunition location and only 12 cartridges qualified as such, with all the rest under the compartment floor. Machine-gun ammo totaled 7,500 rounds. In addition, the machine-gun cupola required redesign for better ventilation. On the positive side, the 32-pdr tracers were visible to 2,926m and barrel life was classified as "long." If stowage could be improved, a rate of fire of six to eight rounds per minute could have been accomplished by the two loaders. Smoke screening equipment was generous, including a 2in trainable mortar and three six-tube self-screening smoke projectors.

Today, one Tortoise may be seen in running condition at the Tank Museum, Bovington, a most impressive accomplishment. It was last used in firing trials at Larkhill in 1949. One other is hulked at the Kirkcudbright military training area in Scotland, probably not restorable.

This plan shows the tight fit of the seven-man crew in the confines of the fighting compartment, and why there was so little ammunition stowed above the floor. The gun took up considerable space even though the fighting compartment extended over the tracks on each side. Lower-right view shows the commander and the front machine gunner (the 32-pdr gunner sat between him and the gun mount). Next above are the driver and the cupola machine gunner. Not shown are the two loaders, up against the rear wall. (Photo The Tank Museum, Bovington)

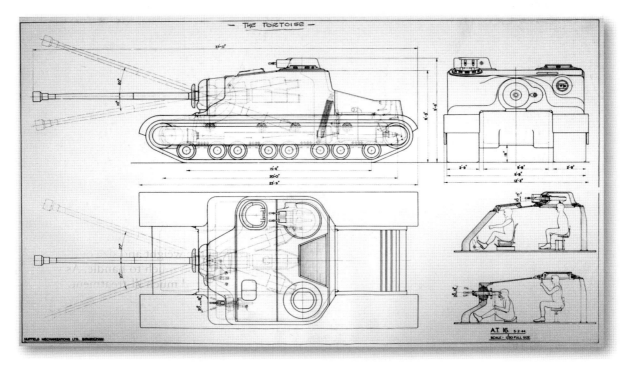

- THE TORTOISE -

# SUMMARY

Although primarily a history of multiple failures, the super-heavy tanks of World War II provided a multitude of challenges to the engineering problems of tank design and manufacture, and several technological exploits resulted from the experience of bringing them to the final stages. In most cases, however, the sheer size and weight of these vehicles exceeded the available technologies and manufacturing capabilities.

These setbacks proved no specific undoing for the armies concerned, despite the sheer waste of materials one might consider they involved. The numbers attempted remained very small. Above all, the tactical and operational considerations that brought them into development were proven false or obsolete by the time they could have entered service. Fortifications of all kinds and power were encountered and overcome in World War II without the use of specialized armored vehicles. The accomplishment of tactical and operational breakthrough on the modern battlefield came to depend more on numbers, mobility, and logistical sustainment than the application of superior guns and armor at a single point. The minor experiences of German operations with their Jagdtiger tank destroyers pointed out that when not employed in substantial numbers, super-heavy tanks were soon overwhelmed and swept aside in the Allied advances.

Above all, the logistical handicaps of the super-heavies presaged their doom. The operational constraints posed by at least partial disassembly for rail transport, the limitations of bridging and fording means, and the ever existent possibility of miring in swamps or even city streets that their high length-to-width steering profiles could carve up all made for extraordinary difficulties. Left to their own automotive power for deployment, they could not hold up for long under constant stressing of barely tested components. The armies learned well from these experiences and nothing of their like ever again roamed the earth, except for some highly specialized engineering and construction equipment.

# FURTHER READING

Devey, Andrew, *Jagdtiger: the Most Powerful Armored Fighting Vehicle of World War II*, 2 vols (Schiffer, 1999)

Ferrand, Stéphan, *Histoire des Blindés Français* (Argos, 2012)

Frölich, Michael, *Kampfpanzer Maus: der Überschwere Panzer Porsche Typ 205* (Motorbuch, 2013).

HaraTomio, Denji Eimori and Akira Takizawa, *Japanese Tanks* (Shuppan-Kyodo, 1978)

Harris, J. P., *Men, Ideas and Tanks: British Military Thought and Armoured Forces, 1903–1939* (Manchester University, 1996)

Hunnicutt, Richard P., *Firepower: A History of the American Heavy Tank* (Presidio, 1988)

Jentz, Thomas L., *Panzerkampfwagen Maus* (Darlington, 1997)

Jentz, Thomas L. and Hilary Louis Doyle, *Schwere Panzerkampfwagen Maus and E100: Development and Production from 1942 to 1945* (Panzer Tracts, 2008)

Kolomiets, M. and V. Mal'ginov, *Soviet Supertanks* (Bronekollektsiya (Armour Collection) No. 1, 2002)

Closer detail of the Tortoise gun mount shows the unique gimbal mounting of the 32-pdr cannon. The gun fired a 14.5kg capped armor-piercing round at a muzzle velocity of 945m/sec. (Author photo)

Malmassari, Paul, "Les Projets de Chars de Forteresse, " *Revue Historique des Armées*, 1 (2004), 11–24

Musée des Blindes, *Le Char 2C* (Saumur Muséum, n.d.)

Sayama, Jiro, *Japanese Army Cannons: Heavy Field Cannons, Cavalry Cannons, and more* (Kojinsha, 2012)

Schneider, Wolfgang and Rainer Strasheim, *Deutsche Kampfwagen im 1. Weltkrieg. Der A7V und die Anfänge deutscher Panzerentwicklung (Das Waffen-Arsenal. Band 112)* (Podzun-Pallas, 1988)

Shigeo, Otaka, "Story on the Secret Development of the Moving Pillbox Phantom, the 100-ton Tank," in Toyosaku Shimada (ed), *Tank and Tank Battles* (Kojinsha, 2012)

Shin Okuda,Reo Kei,Michihiko Saitō,Morihiro Matsudai, *Imperial Japanese Army Ground Weapon Guide 1872-1945* (Shinkigensha, 1997)

Spielberger, Walter J., Hilary L. Doyle, and Thomas L. Jentz, *Heavy Jagdpanzer* (Schiffer, 2007)

Svirin, Mikhail, *Soviet Tank Artillery, 1940–1945* (Armada, 1997)

United Kingdom. "Development of New Series German Tanks up to the end of March, 1945," *Combined Intelligence Objectives Sub-Committee 19:XXXII:35*. [Available from Fox Company Research http://foxcompanyresearch.photodeck.com/]

Zaloga, Steven J., *German Panzers 1914–18* (Osprey, 2006)

Zaloga, Steven J. and James Grandsen, *Soviet Tanks and Combat Vehicles of World War II* (Arms and Armour, 1984)

# INDEX

Page references in **bold** refer to photographs and captions.